HABIT

HABIT[1]

WHEN we look at living creatures from an outward point of view, one of the first things that strike us is that they are bundles of habits. In wild animals, the usual round of daily behavior seems a necessity implanted at birth. in animals domesticated, and especially in man, it seems, to a great extent, to be the result of education. The habits to which there is an innate tendency are called instincts; some of those due to education would by most persons be called acts of reason. It thus appears that habit covers a very large part of life, and that one engaged in studying the objective manifestations of mind is

[1] This chapter has already appeared in the Popular Science Monthly for February 1887.

bound at the very outset to define clearly just what its limits are.

The moment one tries to define what habit is, one is led to the fundamental properties of matter. The laws of Nature are nothing but the immutable habits which the different elementary sorts of matter follow in their actions and reactions upon each other. In the organic world, however, the habits are more variable than this. Even instincts vary from one individual to another of a kind; and are modified in the same individual, as we shall later see, to suit the exigencies of the case. The habits of an elementary particle of matter cannot change (on the principles of the atomistic philosophy), because the particle is itself an unchangeable thing; but those of a compound mass of matter can change, because they are in the last instance due to the structure of the compound, and either outward forces or inward tensions can, from one hour to another, turn that structure into something different from what it was. That is, they can do so if the body be plastic enough to maintain its integrity, and be not disrupted when its structure yields. The change of structure here spoken of need not involve the outward shape; it may be invisible and molecular, as when a bar of iron becomes magnetic or crystalline through the action of certain outward causes, or India-rubber becomes friable, or plaster 'sets.' All these changes are rather slow; the material in question opposes a certain resistance to the modifying cause, which it takes time to overcome, but the gradual yielding whereof often saves the material from being disintegrated altogether. When the structure has yielded, the same inertia becomes a condition of its comparative permanence in the new form, and of the new habits the body then manifests. *Plasticity*, then, in the wide sense of the word, means the possession of a structure weak enough to yield to an influence, but strong enough not to yield all at once. Each relatively stable phase of equilibrium in such a structure is marked by what we may call a new set of habits. Organic matter, especially nervous tissue, seems endowed with a very extraordinary degree of plasticity of this sort; so that we may without hesitation lay down as our first proposition the following, that *the phenomena of habit in living beings are due to the plasticity[1] of the organic materials of which their bodies are composed.*

But the philosophy of habit is thus, in the first instance, a chapter in physics rather than in physiology or psychology. That it is at bottom a physical principle is admitted by all good recent writers on the subject.

[1] In the sense above explained, which applies to inner structure as well as to outer form.

They call attention to analogues of acquired habits exhibited by dead matter. Thus M. Leon Dumont, whose essay on habit is perhaps the most philosophical account yet published, writes:

"Every one knows how a garment, after having been worn a certain time, clings to the shape of the body better than when it was new; there has been a change in the tissue, and this change is a new habit of cohesion. A lock works better after being used some time; at the outset more force was required to overcome certain roughnesses in the mechanism. The overcoming of their resistance is a phenomenon of habituation. It costs less trouble to fold a paper when it has been folded already. This saving of trouble is due to the essential nature of habit, which brings it about that, to reproduce the effect, a less amount of the outward cause is required. The sounds of a violin improve by use in the hands of an able artist, because the fibres of the wood at last contract habits of vibration conformed to harmonic relations. This is what gives such inestimable value to instruments that have belonged to great masters. Water, in flowing, hollows out for itself a channel, which grows broader and deeper; and, after having ceased to flow, it resumes, when it flows again, the path traced by itself before. Just so, the impressions of outer objects fashion for themselves in the nervous system more and more appropriate paths, and these vital phenomena recur under similar excitements from without, when they have been interrupted a certain time." [1]

Not in the nervous system alone. A scar anywhere is a *locus minoris resistentiæ*, more

[1] Revue Philosophique, I, 324.

liable to be abraded, inflamed, to suffer pain and cold, than are the neighboring parts. A sprained ankle, a dislocated arm, are in danger of being sprained or dislocated again; joints that have once been attacked by rheumatism or gout, mucous membranes that have been the seat of catarrh, are with each fresh recurrence more prone to a relapse, until often the morbid state chronically substitutes itself for the sound one. And if we ascend to the nervous system, we find how many so-called functional diseases seem to keep themselves going simply because they happen to have once begun; and how the forcible cutting short by medicine of a few attacks is often sufficient to enable the physiological forces to get possession of the field again, and to bring the organs back to functions of health. Epilepsies, neuralgias, convulsive affections of various sorts, insomnias, are so many cases in point. And, to take what are more obviously habits, the success with which a 'weaning' treatment can often be applied to the victims of unhealthy indulgence of passion, or of mere complaining or irascible disposition, shows us how much the morbid manifestations themselves were due to the mere inertia of the nervous organs, when once launched on a false career.

Can we now form a notion of what the inward physical changes may be like, in organs whose habits have thus struck into new paths? In other words, can we say just what mechanical facts the expression 'change of habit' covers when it is applied to a nervous system? Certainly we cannot in anything like a minute or definite way. But our usual scientific custom of interpreting hidden molecular events after the analogy of visible massive ones enables us to frame easily an abstract and general scheme of processes which the physical changes in question *may* be like. And when once the possibility of *some* kind of mechanical interpretation is established, Mechanical Science, in her present mood, will not hesitate to set her brand of ownership upon the matter, feeling sure that it is only a question of time when the exact mechanical explanation of the case shall be found out.

If habits are due to the plasticity of materials to outward agents, we can immediately see to what outward influences, if to any, the brain-matter is plastic. Not to mechanical pressures, not to thermal changes, not to any of the forces to which all the other organs of our body are exposed; for nature has carefully shut up our brain and spinal cord in bony boxes, where no influences of this sort can get at them. She has floated them in fluid so that only the severest shocks can give them a concussion, and blanketed and wrapped them about in an altogether exceptional way. The only impressions that can be made upon them are through the blood, on the one hand, and through the sensory nerve-roots, on the other; and it is to the infinitely attenuated currents that pour in through these latter channels that the hemispherical cortex shows itself to be so peculiarly susceptible. The currents, once in, must find a way out. In getting out they leave their traces in the paths which they take. The only thing they *can* do, in short, is to deepen old paths or to make new ones; and the whole plasticity of the brain sums itself up in two words when we call it an organ in which currents pouring in from the sense-organs make with extreme facility paths which do not easily disappear. For, of course, a simple habit, like every other nervous event—the habit of snuffling, for example, or of putting one's hands into one's pockets, or of biting one's nails—is, mechanically, nothing but a reflex discharge; and its anatomical substratum must be a path in the system. The most complex habits, as we shall presently see more fully, are, from the same point of view, nothing but *concatenated* discharges in the nerve-centres, due to the presence there of systems of reflex paths, so organized as to wake each other up successively—the impression produced by one muscular contraction serving as a stimulus to provoke the next, until a final impression inhibits the process and closes the chain. The only difficult mechanical problem is to explain the formation *de novo* of a simple reflex or path in a pre-existing nervous system. Here, as in so many other cases, it is only the *premier pas qui coûte*. For the entire nervous system *is* nothing but a system of paths between a sensory *terminus a quo* and a muscular, glandular, or other *terminus ad quem.* A path once traversed by a nerve-current might be expected to follow the law of most of the paths we know, and to be scooped out and made more permeable than before; [1] and this ought to be repeated with each new passage of the current. Whatever obstructions may have kept it at first from being a path should then, little by little, and more and more, be swept out of the way, until at last it might become a natural drainage-channel. This is what happens where either solids or liquids pass over a path; there seems no reason why it should not happen where the thing that passes is a mere wave of rearrangement in matter that does not displace itself, but merely changes chemically or turns itself round in place, or vibrates across the line. The most plausible views of the nerve-current make it

[1] Some paths, to be sure, are banked up by bodies moving through them under too great pressure, and made impervious. These special cases we disregard.

out to be the passage of some such wave of rearrangement as this. If only a part of the matter of the path were to 'rearrange' itself, the neighboring parts remaining inert, it is easy to see how their inertness might oppose a friction which it would take many waves of rearrangement to break down and overcome. If we call the path itself the 'organ,' and the wave of rearrangement the 'function,' then it is obviously a case for repeating the celebrated French formula of '*La fonction fait l'organe.*'

So nothing is easier than to imagine how, when a current once has traversed a path, it should traverse it more readily still a second time. But what made it ever tra-

---

[1] We cannot say *the will*, for, though many, perhaps most, human habits were once voluntary actions, no action, as we shall see in a later chapter, can be *primarily* such. While an habitual action may once have been voluntary, the voluntary action must before that, at least once, have been impulsive or reflex. It is this very first occurrence of all that we consider in the text.

verse it the first time?[1] In answering this
question we can only fall back on our general
conception of a nervous system as a mass of
matter whose parts, constantly kept in states
of different tension, are as constantly tending
to equalize their states. The equalization
between any two points occurs through whatever path may at the moment be most per-
vious. But, as a given point of the system
may belong, actually or potentially, to many
different paths, and, as the play of nutrition
is subject to accidental changes, *blocks* may
from time to time occur, and make currents
shoot through unwonted lines. Such an
unwonted line would be a new-created path,
which if traversed repeatedly, would become
the beginning of a new reflex arc. All this
is vague to the last degree, and amounts to
little more than saying that a new path may
be formed by the sort of *chances* that in
nervous material are likely to occur. But,

vague as it is, it is really the last word of our wisdom in the matter.[1]

It must be noticed that the growth of structural modification in living matter may be more rapid than in any lifeless mass because the incessant nutritive renovation of which the living matter is the seat tends often to corroborate and fix the impressed modification, rather than to counteract it by renewing the original constitution of the tissue that has been impressed. Thus, we notice after exercising our muscles or our brain in a new way, that we can do so no longer at that time;

---

[1] Those who desire a more definite formulation may consult J. Fiske's 'Cosmic Philosophy,' vol. II. pp.142–146, and Spencer's 'Principles of Biology,' sections 302 and 303, and the part entitled 'Physical Synthesis' of his 'Principles of Psychology.' Mr. Spencer there tries, not only to show how new actions may arise in nervous systems and form new reflex arcs therein, but even how nervous tissue may actually be born by the passage of new waves of isometric transformation through an originally indifferent mass. I cannot help thinking that Mr. Spencer's data, under a great show of precision, conceal vagueness and improbability, and even self-contradiction.

but after a day or two of rest, when we resume the discipline, our increase in skill not seldom surprises us. I have often noticed this in learning a tune; and it has led a German author to say that we learn to swim during the winter and to skate during the summer.

Dr. Carpenter writes: [1]

"It is a matter of universal experience that every kind of training for special aptitudes is both far more effective, and leaves a more permanent impress, when exerted on the *growing* organism than when brought to bear on the adult. The effect of such training is shown in the tendency of the organ to 'grow to' the mode in which it is habitually exercised; as is evidenced by the increased size and power of particular sets of muscles, and the extraordinary flexibility of joints, which are acquired by such as have been

[1] 'Mental Physiology' (1874), pp. 339–345.

early exercised in gymnastic performances.
. . . There is no part of the organism of
man in which the *reconstructive activity* is so
great, during the whole period of life, as it
is in the ganglionic substance of the brain.
This is indicated by the enormous supply of
blood which it receives. . . . It is, moreover, a fact of great significance that the
nerve-substance is specially distinguished by
its *reparative* power. For while injuries of
other tissues (such as the muscular) which
are distinguished by the *speciality* of their
structure and endowments, are repaired by
substance of a lower or less specialized type,
those of nerve-substance are repaired by a
complete reproduction of the normal tissue;
as is evidenced in the sensibility of the newly
forming skin which is closing over an open
wound, or in the recovery of the sensibility
of a piece of 'transplanted' skin, which has
for a time been rendered insensible by the

complete interruption of the continuity of its nerves. The most remarkable example of this reproduction, however, is afforded by the results of M. Brown-Séquard's [1] experiments upon the gradual restoration of the functional activity of the spinal cord after its complete division; which takes place in a way that indicates rather a *reproduction* of the whole, or the lower part of the cord and of the nerves proceeding from it, than a mere *reunion* of divided surfaces. This reproduction is but a special manifestation of the reconstructive change which is *always* taking place in the nervous system; it being not less obvious to the eye of reason that the 'waste' occasioned by its functional activity must be constantly repaired by the production of new tissue, than it is to the eye of sense that such reparation supplies an

[1] [See, later, Masius in Van Benedens' and Van Bambeke's 'Archives de Biologie,' vol I (Liége 1880).—W. J.]

actual *loss* of substance by disease or injury.

"Now, in this constant and active reconstruction of the nervous system, we recognize a most marked conformity to the general plan manifested in the nutrition of the organism as a whole. For, in the first place, it is obvious that there is a tendency to the production of a *determinate type* of structure; which type is often not merely that of the species, but some special modification of it which characterized one or both of the progenitors. But this type is peculiarly liable to modification during the early period of life; in which the functional activity of the nervous system (and particularly of the brain) is extraordinarily great, and the reconstructive process proportionally active. And this modifiability expresses itself in the formation of the mechanism by which those *secondarily automatic* modes of movement

come to be established, which, in man, take
the place of those that are *congenital* in most
of the animals beneath him; and those modes
of sense-perception come to be *acquired*
which are elsewhere clearly *instinctive.* For
there can be no reasonable doubt that, in
both cases, a nervous mechanism is *developed*
in the course of this self-education, corre-
sponding with that which the lower animals
inherit from their parents. The *plan* of that
rebuilding process, which is necessary to maintain the integrity of the organism generally,
and which goes on with peculiar activity in
this portion of it, is thus being incessantly
modified; and in this manner all that portion
of it which ministers to the *external* life of
sense and motion that is shared by man with
the animal kingdom at large, becomes at adult
age the expression of the habits which the
individual has acquired during the period of
growth and development. Of these habits,

some are common to the race generally, while others are peculiar to the individual; those of the former kind (such as walking erect) being universally acquired, save where physical inability prevents; while for the latter a special training is needed, which is usually the more effective the earlier it is begun—as is remarkably seen in the case of such feats of dexterity as require a conjoint education of the perceptive and of the motor powers. And when thus developed during the period of growth, so as to have become a part of the constitution of the adult, the acquired mechanism is thenceforth maintained in the ordinary course of the nutritive operations, so as to be ready for use when called upon, even after long inaction.

"What is so clearly true of the nervous apparatus of animal life can scarcely be otherwise than true of that which ministers to the automatic activity of the mind. For,

as already shown, the study of psychology
has evolved no more certain result than that
there are uniformities of mental action which
are so entirely conformable to those of bodily
action as to indicate their intimate relation
to a 'mechanism of thought and feeling,'
acting under the like conditions with that of
sense and motion. The psychical principles
of *association*, indeed, and the physiological
principles of *nutrition*, simply express—the
former in terms of mind, the latter in terms
of brain—the universally admitted fact that
any sequence of mental action which has
been frequently repeated tends to perpetuate
itself; so that we find ourselves automatically
prompted to *think*, *feel*, or *do* what we have
been before accustomed to think, feel, or do,
under like circumstances, without any con-
sciously formed *purpose*, or anticipation of
results. For there is no reason to regard the
cerebrum as an exception to the general

principle that, while each part of the organism tends to *form itself* in accordance with the mode in which it is habitually exercised, this tendency will be especially strong in the nervous apparatus, in virtue of that *incessant regeneration* which is the very condition of its functional activity. It scarcely, indeed, admits of doubt that every state of ideational consciousness which is either *very strong* or is *habitually repeated* leaves an organic impression on the cerebrum; in virtue of which that same state may be reproduced at any future time, in respondence to a suggestion fitted to excite it. . . . The 'strength of early association' is a fact so universally recognized that the expression of it has become proverbial; and this precisely accords with the physiological principle that, during the period of growth and development, the formative activity of the brain will be most amenable to directing influences. It is in this way that what is early 'learned by heart' becomes branded in (as it were) upon the cerebrum; so that its 'traces' are never lost, even though the conscious memory of it may have completely faded out. For, when the organic modification has been once *fixed* in the growing brain, it becomes a part of the normal fabric, and is regularly *maintained* by nutritive substitution; so that it may endure to the end of life, like the scar of a wound."

Dr. Carpenter's phrase that *our nervous system grows to the modes in which it has been exercised* expresses the philosophy of habit in a nutshell. We may now trace some of the practical applications of the principle to human life.

The first result of it is that *habit simplifies the movements required to achieve a given result, makes them more accurate and diminishes fatigue.*

"The beginner at the piano not only moves his finger up and down in order to depress the key, he moves the whole hand, the forearm and even the entire body, especially moving its least rigid part, the head, as if he would press down the key with that organ too. Often a contraction of the abdominal muscles occurs as well. Principally, however, the impulse is determined to the motion of the hand and of the single finger. This is, in the first place, because the movement of the finger is the movement *thought of*, and, in the second place, because its movement and that of the key are the movements we try to *perceive*, along with the results of the latter on the ear. The more often the process is repeated, the more easily the movement follows, on account of the increase in permeability of the nerves engaged.

"But the more easily the movement occurs, the slighter is the stimulus required to set it up; and the slighter the stimulus is, the more its effect is confined to the fingers alone.

"Thus, an impulse which originally spread its effects over the whole body, or at least over many of its movable parts, is gradually determined to a single definite organ, in which it effects the contraction of a few limited muscles.   In this change the thoughts and perceptions which start the impulse acquire more and more intimate causal relations with a particular group of motor nerves.

"To recur to a simile, at least partially apt, imagine the nervous system to represent a drainage-system, inclining, on the whole, toward certain muscles, but with the escape thither somewhat clogged.   Then streams of water will, on the whole, tend most to fill the drains that go toward these muscles and to wash out the escape.   In case of a sudden 'flushing,' however, the whole system of channels will fill itself, and the water overflow everywhere before it escapes. But a moderate quantity of water invading the system will flow through the proper escape alone.

"Just so with the piano-player. As soon as his impulse, which has gradually learned to confine itself to single muscles, grows extreme, it overflows into larger muscular regions. He usually plays with his fingers, his body being at rest. But no sooner does he get excited than his whole body becomes 'animated,' and he moves his head and trunk, in particular, as if these also were organs with which he meant to belabor the keys." [1]

Man is born with a tendency to do more things than he has ready-made arrangements for in his nerve-centres. Most of the performances of other animals are automatic. But in him the number of them is so enor-

[1] G. H. Schneider: 'Der menschliche Wille' (1882), pp. 417–419 (freely translated). For the drain-simile, see also Spencer's 'Psychology,' part V, chap. VIII.

mous, that most of them must be the fruit of painful study. If practice did not make perfect, nor habit economize the expense of nervous and muscular energy, he would therefore be in a sorry plight. As Dr. Maudsley says:[1]

"If an act became no easier after being done several times, if the careful direction of consciousness were necessary to its accomplishment on each occasion, it is evident that the whole activity of a lifetime might be confined to one or two deeds—that no progress could take place in development. A man might be occupied all day in dressing and undressing himself; the attitude of his body would absorb all his attention and energy; the washing of his hands or the fastening of a button would be as difficult to him on each occasion as to the child on

[1] 'Physiology of Mind,' p. 155.

its first trial; and he would, furthermore, be completely exhausted by his exertions. Think of the pains necessary to teach a child to stand, of the many efforts which it must make, and of the ease with which it at last stands, unconscious of any effort. For while secondarily automatic acts are accomplished with comparatively little weariness—in this regard approaching the organic movements, or the original reflex movements—the conscious effort of the will soon produces exhaustion. A spinal cord without . . . memory would simply be an idiotic spinal cord. . . . It is impossible for an individual to realize how much he owes to its automatic agency until disease has impaired its functions."

The next result is that *habit diminishes the conscious attention with which our acts are performed.*

One may state this abstractly thus: If
an act require for its execution a chain,
A, B, C, D, E, F, G, etc., of successive
nervous events, then in the first performances
of the action the conscious will must choose;
each of these events from a number of wrong
alternatives that tend to present themselves;
but habit soon brings it about that each
event calls up its own appropriate successor
without any alternative offering itself, and
without any reference to the conscious will,
until at last the whole chain, *A, B, C, D, E,
F, G*, rattles itself off as soon as *A* occurs,
just as if *A* and the rest of the chain were
fused into a continuous stream. When we
are learning to walk, to ride, to swim, skate,
fence, write, play, or sing, we interrupt ourselves at every step by unnecessary movements and false notes. When we are pro-
ficients, on the contrary, the results not only
follow with the very minimum of muscular

action requisite to bring them forth, they also follow from a single instantaneous 'cue.' The marksman sees the bird, and, before he knows it, he has aimed and shot. A gleam in his adversary's eye, a momentary pressure from his rapier, and the fencer finds that he has instantly made the right parry and return. A glance at the musical hieroglyphics, and the pianist's fingers have ripped through a cataract of notes. And not only is it the right thing at the right time that we thus involuntarily do, but the wrong thing also, if it be an habitual thing. Who is there that has never wound up his watch on taking off his waistcoat in the daytime, or taken his latch-key out on arriving at the door-step of a friend? Very absent-minded persons in going to their bedroom to dress for dinner have been known to take off one garment after another and finally to get into bed, merely because that was the habitual issue of the first few movements when performed at a later hour. The writer well remembers how, on revisiting Paris after ten years' absence, and, finding himself in the street in which for one winter he had attended school, he lost himself in a brown study, from which he was awakened by finding himself upon the stairs which led to the apartment in a house many streets away in which he had lived during that earlier time, and to which his steps from the school had then habitually led. We all of us have a definite routine manner of performing certain daily offices connected with the toilet, with the opening and shutting of familiar cupboards, and the like. Our lower centres know the order of these movements, and show their knowledge by their 'surprise' if the objects are altered so as to oblige the movement to be made in a different way. But our higher thought-centres know hardly anything about the matter. Few men can tell off-hand which sock, shoe, or trousers-leg they put on first. They must first mentally rehearse the act; and even that is often insufficient—the act must be *performed*. So of the questions, Which valve of my double door opens first? Which way does my door swing? etc. I cannot *tell* the answer; yet my *hand* never makes a mistake. No one can *describe* the order in which he brushes his hair or teeth; yet it is likely that the order is a pretty fixed one in all of us.

These results may be expressed as follows:

In action grown habitual, what instigates each new muscular contraction to take place in its appointed order is not a thought or a perception, but the *sensation occasioned by the muscular contraction just finished*. A strictly voluntary act has to be guided by idea, perception, and volition, throughout its whole course. In an habitual action, mere sensation is a sufficient guide, and the upper regions of brain and mind are set comparatively free. A diagram will make the matter clear:

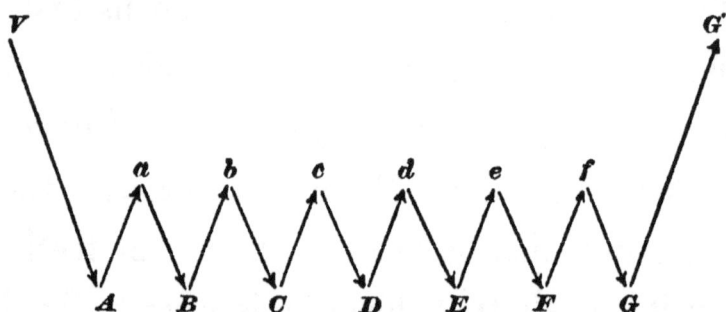

Let A, B, C, D, E, F, G represent an habitual chain of muscular contractions, and let a, b, c, d, e, f stand for the respective sensations which these contractions excite in us when they are successfully performed. Such sensations will usually be of the muscles, skin, or joints of the parts moved, but they may also be effects of the movement upon the eye or the ear. Through them, and through them alone, we are made aware whether the contraction has or has not occurred. When the series, A, B, C, D, E, F, G, is being learned, each of these sensations becomes the object of a separate perception by the mind. By it we test each movement, to see if it be right before advancing to the next. We hesitate, compare, choose, revoke, reject, etc., by intellectual means; and the order by which the next movement is discharged is an express order from the ideational centres after this deliberation has been gone through.

In habitual action, on the contrary, the only impulse which the centres of idea or perception need send down is the initial impulse, the command to *start*. This is represented in the diagram by V; it may be a thought of the first movement or of the last result, or a mere perception of some of the habitual conditions of the chain, the presence, e.g., of the keyboard near the hand. In the present case, no sooner has the conscious thought or volition instigated movement A, than A, through the sensation a of its own occurrence, awakens B reflexly; B then excites C through b, and so on till the chain is ended, when the intellect generally takes cognizance of the final result. The process, in fact, resembles the passage of a wave of 'peristaltic' motion down the bowels. The intellectual perception at the end is indicated in the diagram by the effect of G being represented, at G^1, in the ideational centres above the merely sensational line. The sensational impressions, a, b, c, d, e, f, are all supposed to have their seat below the ideational lines. That our ideational centres, if involved at all by a, b, c, d, e, f, are involved in a minimal degree, is shown by the fact that the attention may be wholly absorbed elsewhere. We may say our prayers, or repeat the alphabet, with our attention far away.

"A musical performer will play a piece which has become familiar by repetition while carrying on an animated conversation or while continuously engrossed by some train of deeply interesting thought; the accustomed sequence of movements being directly prompted by the *sight* of the notes, or by the remembered succession of the *sounds* (if the piece is played from memory), aided in both cases by the guiding sensations derived from the muscles themselves. But, further, a higher degree of the same 'training' (acting on an organism specially fitted to profit by it) enables an accomplished pianist to play a difficult piece of music at sight; the movements of the hands and fingers following so immediately upon the sight of the notes that it seems impossible to believe that any but the very shortest and most direct track can be the channel of the nervous communication through which they are called forth.

The following curious example of the same class of *acquired aptitudes*, which differ from instincts only in being prompted to action by the will, is furnished by Robert Houdin:

"'With a view of cultivating the rapidity of visual and tactile perception, and the precision of respondent movements, which are necessary for success in every kind of prestidigitation, Houdin early practised the art of juggling with balls in the air; and having, after a month's practice, become thorough master of the art of keeping up *four* balls at once, he placed a book before him, and, while the balls were in the air, accustomed himself to read without hesitation. 'This,' he says, 'will probably seem to my readers very extraordinary; but I shall surprise them still more when I say that I have just amused myself with repeating this curious experiment. Though thirty years have elapsed since the time I was writing, and though I have scarcely once touched the balls during that period, I can still manage to read with ease while keeping *three* balls up.'" (Autobiography, p. 26.)[1]

We have called *a, b, c, d, e, f,* the antecedents of the successive muscular attractions, by the name of sensations. Some authors seem to deny that they are even this. If not even this, they can only be centripetal nerve-currents, not sufficient to arouse feeling, but sufficient to arouse motor response.[2] It may be at once admitted that they are not distinct *volitions.* The will, if any will be present, limits itself to a *permission* that they exert their motor effects. Dr. Carpenter writes:

"There may still be metaphysicians who

[1] Carpenter's 'Mental Physiology' (1874), pp. 217, 218.

[2] Von Hartmann devotes a chapter of his 'Philosophy of the Unconscious' (English translation, vol. I. p. 72) to proving that they must be both *ideas* and *unconscious.*

maintain that actions which were originally
prompted by the will with a distinct inten-
tion, and which are still entirely under its
control, can never cease to be volitional;
and that either an infinitesimally small
amount of will is required to sustain them
when they have been once set going, or that
the will is in a sort of pendulum-like oscillation between the two actions—the mainte-
nance of the train of *thought*, and the mainte-
nance of the train of *movement*. But if only
an infinitesimally small amount of will is
necessary to sustain them, is not this tanta-
mount to saying that they go on by a force
of their own? And does not the experience
of the *perfect continuity* of our train of thought
during the performance of movements that
have become habitual, entirely negative the
hypothesis of oscillation? Besides, if such
an oscillation existed, there must be *intervals*
in which each action goes on *of itself;* so that

its essentially automatic character is vir-
tually admitted. The physiological explanation, that the mechanism of locomotion, as
of habitual movements, *grows to* the mode
in which it is early exercised, and that it then
works automatically under the general control and direction of the will, can scarcely
be put down by any assumption of an hypo-
thetical necessity, which rests only on the
basis of ignorance of one side of our composite
nature." [1]

But if not distinct acts of will, these im-
mediate antecedents of each movement of
the chain are at any rate accompanied by consciousness of some kind. They are *sensations* to which we are *usually inattentive*, but
which immediately call our attention if they
go *wrong*. Schneider's account of these
sensations deserves to be quoted. In the

[1] 'Mental Physiology,' p. 20.

act of walking, he says, even when our attention is entirely off,

"we are continuously aware of certain muscular feelings; and we have, moreover, a
feeling of certain impulses to keep our
equilibrium and to set down one leg after
another. It is doubtful whether we could
preserve equilibrium if no sensation of our
body's attitude were there, and doubtful
whether we should advance our leg if we had
no sensation of its movement as executed,
and not even a minimal feeling of impulse
to set it down. Knitting appears altogether
mechanical, and the knitter keeps up her
knitting even while she reads or is engaged in
lively talk. But if we ask her how this be
possible, she will hardly reply that the
knitting goes on of itself. She will rather
say that she has a feeling of it, that she
feels in her hands that she knits and

how she must knit, and that therefore the movements of knitting are called forth and regulated by the sensations associated therewithal even when the attention is called away.

"So of every one who practises, apparently automatically, a long-familiar handicraft. The smith turning his tongs as he smites the iron, the carpenter wielding his plane, the lace-maker with her bobbin, the weaver at his loom, all will answer the same question in the same way by saying that they have a feeling of the proper management of the implement in their hands.

"In these cases, the feelings which are conditions of the appropriate acts are very faint. But none the less are they necessary. Imagine your hands not feeling; your movements could then only be provoked by ideas, and if your ideas were then diverted away, the movements ought to come to a standstill, which is a consequence that seldom occurs."[1]

Again:

"An idea makes you take, for example, a violin into your left hand. But it is not necessary that your idea remain fixed on the contraction of the muscles of the left hand and fingers in order that the violin may continue to be held fast and not let fall. The sensations themselves which the holding of the instrument awakens in the hand, since they are associated with the motor impulse of grasping, are sufficient to cause this impulse, which then lasts as long as the feeling itself lasts, or until the impulse is inhibited by the idea of some antagonistic motion." And the same may be said of the manner in which the right hand holds the bow:

[1] 'Der menschliche Wille,' pp. 447, 448.

"It sometimes happens, in beginning these simultaneous combinations, that one movement or impulse will cease if the consciousness turn particularly toward another, because at the outset the guiding sensations must *all* be strongly *felt*. The bow will perhaps slip from the fingers, because some of the muscles have relaxed. But the slipping is a cause of new sensations starting up in the hand, so that the attention is in a moment brought back to the grasping of the bow.

"The following experiment shows this well: When one begins to play on the violin, to keep him from raising his right elbow in playing a book is placed under his right armpit, which he is ordered to hold fast by keeping the upper arm tight against his body. The muscular feelings, and feelings of contact connected with the book, provoke an impulse to press it tight. But often it happens that the beginner, whose attention gets absorbed in the production of the notes, lets drop the book. Later, however, this never happens; the faintest sensations of contact suffice to awaken the impulse to keep it in its place, and the attention may be wholly absorbed by the notes and the fingering with the left hand. *The simultaneous combination of movements is thus in the first instance conditioned by the facility with which in us, alongside of intellectual processes, processes of inattentive feeling may still go on.*" [1]

This brings us by a very natural transition to the *ethical implications of the law of habit.* They are numerous and momentous. Dr. Carpenter, from whose 'Mental Physiology' we have quoted, has so prominently enforced the principle that our organs grow to the way in which they have been exercised, and dwelt

[1] 'Der menschliche Wille,' p. 439. The last sentence is rather freely translated—the sense is unaltered.

upon its consequences, that his book almost deserves to be called a work of edification, on this account alone. We need make no apology, then, for tracing a few of these consequences ourselves:

"Habit a second nature! Habit is ten times nature," the Duke of Wellington is said to have exclaimed; and the degree to which this is true no one can probably appreciate as well as one who is a veteran soldier himself. The daily drill and the years of discipline end by fashioning a man completely over again, as to most of the possibilities of his conduct.

"There is a story, which is credible enough though it may not be true, of a practical joker, who, seeing a discharged veteran carrying home his dinner, suddenly called out, 'Attention!' whereupon the man instantly brought his hands down, and lost his mutton and potatoes in the gutter. The drill had been thorough, and its effects had become embodied in the man's nervous structure." [1]

Riderless cavalry-horses, at many a battle, have been seen to come together and go through their customary evolutions at the sound of the bugle-call. Most trained domestic animals, dogs and oxen, and omnibus- and car-horses, seem to be machines almost pure and simple, undoubtingly, unhesitatingly doing from minute to minute the duties they have been taught, and giving no sign that the possibility of an alternative ever suggests itself to their mind. Men grown old in prison have asked to be readmitted after being once set free. In a railroad accident to a travelling menagerie in the United States some time in 1884, a tiger, whose cage had broken open, is said to have emerged,

[1] Huxley's 'Elementary Lessons in Physiology,' lesson XII.

but presently crept back again, as if too
much bewildered by his new responsibilities,
so that he was without difficulty secured.

Habit is thus the enormous fly-wheel of
society, its most precious conservative agent.
It alone is what keeps us all within the bounds
of ordinance, and saves the children of for-
tune from the envious uprisings of the poor.
It alone prevents the hardest and most
repulsive walks of life from being deserted
by those brought up to tread therein. It
keeps the fisherman and the deck-hand at
sea through the winter; it holds the miner
in his darkness, and nails the countryman to
his log cabin and his lonely farm through all
the months of snow; it protects us from in-
vasion by the natives of the desert and the
frozen zone. It dooms us all to fight out the
battle of life upon the lines of our nurture
or our early choice, and to make the best
of a pursuit that disagrees, because there is

no other for which we are fitted, and it is too late to begin again. It keeps different social strata from mixing. Already at the age of twenty-five you see the professional mannerism settling down on the young commercial traveller, on the young doctor, on the young minister, on the young counsellor-at-law. You see the little lines of cleavage running through the character, the tricks of thought, the prejudices, the ways of the 'shop,' in a word, from which the man can by-and-by no more escape than his coat-sleeve can suddenly fall into a new set of folds. On the whole, it is best he should not escape. It is well for the world that in most of us, by the age of thirty, the character has set like plaster, and will never soften again.

If the period between twenty and thirty is the critical one in the formation of intellectual and professional habits, the period below twenty is more important still for the fixing of *personal* habits, properly so called, such as vocalization and pronunciation, gesture, motion, and address. Hardly ever is a language learned after twenty spoken without a foreign accent; hardly ever can a youth transferred to the society of his betters unlearn the nasality and other vices of speech bred in him by the associations of his growing years. Hardly ever, indeed, no matter how much money there be in his pocket, can he even learn to *dress* like a gentleman-born. The merchants offer their wares as eagerly to him as to the veriest 'swell,' but he simply *cannot* buy the right things. An invisible law, as strong as gravitation, keeps him within his orbit, arrayed this year as he was the last; and how his better-bred acquaintances contrive to get the things they wear will be for him a mystery till his dying day.

The great thing, then, in all education, is to *make our nervous system our ally instead of our enemy.*   It is to fund and capitalize our acquisitions, and live at ease upon the interest of the fund.   *For this we must make automatic and habitual, as early as possible, as many useful actions as we can,* and guard against the growing into ways that are likely to be disadvantageous to us, as we should guard against the plague.   The more of the details of our daily life we can hand over to the effortless custody of automatism, the more our higher powers of mind will be set free for their own proper work.   There is no more miserable human being than one in whom nothing is habitual but indecision, and for whom the lighting of every cigar, the drinking of every cup, the time of rising and going to bed every day, and the beginning of every bit of work, are subjects of express volitional deliberation.   Full half the time

of such a man goes to the deciding, or regret-
ting, of matters which ought to be so ingrained in him as practically not to exist for
his consciousness at all. If there be such
daily duties not yet ingrained in any one of
my readers, let him begin this very hour to
set the matter right.

In Professor Bain's chapter on 'The Moral
Habits' there are some admirable practical
remarks laid down. Two great maxims
emerge from his treatment. The first is that
in the acquisition of a new habit, or the leav-
ing off of an old one, we must take care to
*launch ourselves with as strong and decided
an initiative as possible.* Accumulate all
the possible circumstances which shall re-
enforce the right motives; put yourself assidu-
ously in conditions that encourage the new
way; make engagements incompatible with
the old; take a public pledge, if the case
allows; in short, envelop your resolution with

every aid you know. This will give your new beginning such a momentum that the temptation to break down will not occur as soon as it otherwise might; and every day during which a breakdown is postponed adds to the chances of its not occurring at all.

The second maxim is: *Never suffer an exception to occur till the new habit is securely rooted in your life.* Each lapse is like the letting fall of a ball of string which one is carefully winding up; a single slip undoes more than a great many turns will wind again. *Continuity* of training is the great means of making the nervous system act infallibly right. As Professor Bain says:

"The peculiarity of the moral habits, contradistinguishing them from the intellectual acquisitions, is the presence of two hostile

powers, one to be gradually raised into the
ascendant over the other. It is necessary,
above all things, in such a situation, never
to lose a battle. Every gain on the wrong
side undoes the effect of many conquests on
the right. The essential precaution, therefore, is so to regulate the two opposing powers
that the one may have a series of uninterrupted successes, until repetition has forti-
fied it to such a degree as to enable it to cope
with the opposition, under any circumstances.
This is the theoretically best career of mental
progress."

The need of securing success at the *outset*
is imperative. Failure at first is apt to
dampen the energy of all future attempts,
whereas past experience of success nerves
one to future vigor. Goethe says to a man
who consulted him about an enterprise but
mistrusted his own powers: "Ach! you

need only blow on your hands!" And the remark illustrates the effect on Goethe's spirits of his own habitually successful career. Prof. Baumann, from whom I borrow the anecdote,[1] says that the collapse of barbarian nations when Europeans come among them is due to their despair of ever succeeding as the new-comers do in the larger tasks of life. Old ways are broken and new ones not formed.

The question of 'tapering-off,' in abandoning such habits as drink and opium-indulgence, comes in here, and is a question about which experts differ within certain limits, and in regard to what may be best for an individual case. In the main, however, all expert opinion would agree that abrupt acquisition of the new habit is the best way, *if there be a real possibility of carrying it out.* We must

---

[1] See the admirable passage about success at the outset, in his 'Handbuch der Moral' (1878), pp. 38-43.

be careful not to give the will so stiff a task as to insure its defeat at the very outset; but, *provided one can stand it*, a sharp period of suffering, and then a free time, is the best thing to aim at, whether in giving up a habit like that of opium, or in simply changing one's hours of rising or of work. It is surprising how soon a desire will die of inanition if it be *never* fed.

"One must first learn, unmoved, looking neither to the right nor left, to walk firmly on the straight and narrow path, before one can begin 'to make one's self over again.' He who every day makes a fresh resolve is like one who, arriving at the edge of the ditch he is to leap, forever stops and returns for a fresh run. Without *unbroken* advance there is no such thing as *accumulation* of the ethical forces possible, and to make this possible, and to exercise us and habituate us in it, is the sovereign blessing of regular *work*." [1]

A third maxim may be added to the preceding pair: *Seize the very first possible opportunity to act on every resolution you make, and on every emotional prompting you may experience in the direction of the habits you aspire to gain.* It is not in the moment of their forming, but in the moment of their producing *motor effects*, that resolves and aspirations communicate the new 'set' to the brain. As the author last quoted remarks:

"The actual presence of the practical opportunity alone furnishes the fulcrum upon which the lever can rest, by means of which the moral will may multiply its

[1] J. Bahnsen: 'Beiträge zu Charakterologie' (1867), vol. I. p. 209.

strength, and raise itself aloft. He who has no solid ground to press against will never get beyond the stage of empty gesture-making."

No matter how full a reservoir of *maxims* one may possess, and no matter how good one's *sentiments* may be, if one have not taken advantage of every concrete opportunity to *act*, one's character may remain entirely unaffected for the better. With mere good intentions, hell is proverbially paved. And this is an obvious consequence of the principles we have laid down. A 'character,' as J.S. Mill says, 'is a completely fashioned will'; and a will, in the sense in which he means it, is an aggregate of tendencies to act in a firm and prompt and definite way upon all the principal emergencies of life. A tendency to act only becomes effectively ingrained in us in proportion to the uninterrupted frequency with which the actions actually occur, and the brain 'grows' to their use. Every time a resolve or a fine glow of feeling evaporates without bearing practical fruit is worse than a chance lost; it works so as positively to hinder future resolutions and emotions from taking the normal path of discharge. There is no more contemptible type of human character than that of the nerveless sentimentalist and dreamer, who spends his life in a weltering sea of sensibility and emotion, but who never does a manly concrete deed. Rousseau, inflaming all the mothers of France, by his eloquence, to follow Nature and nurse their babies themselves, while he sends his own children to the foundling hospital, is the classical example of what I mean. But every one of us in his measure, whenever, after glowing for an abstractly formulated Good, he practically ignores some actual

case, among the squalid 'other particulars'
of which that same Good lurks disguised,
treads straight on Rousseau's path. All
Goods are disguised by the vulgarity of their
concomitants, in this work-a-day world; but
woe to him who can only recognize them
when he thinks them in their pure and
abstract form! The habit of excessive novel-
reading and theatre-going will produce true
monsters in this line. The weeping of a
Russian lady over the fictitious personages
in the play, while her coachman is freezing
to death on his seat outside, is the sort of
thing that everywhere happens on a less
glaring scale. Even the habit of excessive
indulgence in music, for those who are
neither performers themselves nor musically
gifted enough to take it in a purely intellectual way, has probably a relaxing effect upon
the character. One becomes filled with
emotions which habitually pass without

prompting to any deed, and so the inertly sentimental condition is kept up. The remedy would be, never to suffer one's self to have an emotion at a concert, without expressing it afterward in *some* active way.[1] Let the expression be the least thing in the world—speaking genially to one's aunt, or giving up one's seat in a horse-car, if nothing more heroic offers—but let it not fail to take place.

These latter cases make us aware that it is not simply *particular lines* of discharge, but also *general forms* of discharge, that seem to be grooved out by habit in the brain. Just as, if we let our emotions evaporate, they get into a way of evaporating; so there is reason to suppose that if we often flinch from making an effort, before we know it the effort-making capacity will be gone; and that, if we suffer

[1] See for remarks on this subject a readable article by Miss V. Scudder on 'Musical Devotees and Morals,' in the Andover Review for January, 1887.

the wandering of our attention, presently it
will wander all the time. Attention and
effort are, as we shall see later, but two names
for the same psychic fact. To what brain-
processes they correspond we do not know.
The strongest reason for believing that they
do depend on brain-processes at all, and are
not pure acts of the spirit, is just this fact,
that they seem in some degree subject to the
law of habit, which is a material law. As a
final practical maxim, relative to these habits
of the will, we may, then, offer something
like this: *Keep the faculty of effort alive in
you by a little gratuitous exercise every day.*
That is, be systematically ascetic or heroic
in little unnecessary points, do every day or
two something for no other reason than that
you would rather not do it, so that when the
hour of dire need draws nigh, it may find you
not unnerved and untrained to stand the
test. Asceticism of this sort is like the insur-

ance which a man pays on his house and goods. The tax does him no good at the time, and possibly may never bring him a return. But if the fire *does* come, his having paid it will be his salvation from ruin. So with the man who has daily inured himself to habits of concentrated attention, energetic volition, and self-denial in unnecessary things. He will stand like a tower when everything rocks around him, and when his softer fellow-mortals are winnowed like chaff in the blast.

The physiological study of mental conditions is thus the most powerful ally of hortatory ethics. The hell to be endured hereafter, of which theology tells, is no worse than the hell we make for ourselves in this world by habitually fashioning our characters in the wrong way. Could the young but realize how soon they will become mere walking bundles of habits, they would give more heed to their conduct while in the plastic state. We are spinning our own fates, good or evil, and never to be undone. Every smallest stroke of virtue or of vice leaves its never so little scar. The drunken Rip Van Winkle, in Jefferson's play, excuses himself for every fresh dereliction by saying, 'I won't count this time!' Well! he may not count it, and a kind Heaven may not count it; but it is being counted none the less. Down among his nerve-cells and fibres the molecules are counting it, registering and storing it up to be used against him when the next temptation comes. Nothing we ever do is, in strict scientific literalness, wiped out. Of course, this has its good side as well as its bad one. As we become permanent drunkards by so many separate drinks, so we become saints in the moral, and authorities and experts in the practical and scientific spheres, by so many separate acts and hours of work. Let no youth have any anxiety about the upshot of his education, whatever the line of it may be. If he keep faithfully busy each hour of the working-day, he may safely leave the final result to itself. He can with perfect certainty count on waking up some fine morning, to find himself one of the competent ones of his generation, in whatever pursuit he may have singled out. Silently, between all the details of his business, the *power of judging* in all that class of matter will have built itself up within him as a possession that will never pass away. Young people should know this truth in advance. The ignorance of it has probably engendered more discouragement and faint-heartedness in youths embarking on arduous careers than all other causes put together.

www.ingramcontent.com/pod-product-compliance
Lightning Source LLC
Chambersburg PA
CBHW030553270326
41927CB00008B/1628